Megan Rapinoe

CHERRY LAKE PRESS

Published in the United States of America by Cherry Lake Publishing
Ann Arbor, Michigan
www.cherrylakepublishing.com

Reading Adviser: Marla Conn, MS, Ed., Literacy specialist, Read-Ability, Inc.
Book Designer: Jennifer Wahi
Illustrator: Jeff Bane

Photo Credits: © Christopher Pfeifer/Shutterstock, 5; © Niran Movie/Shutterstock, 7; © Zhukovsky/Dreamstime.com, 9; © Jacqueline Cassll/WikiMedia, 11; © Jay Solomon/WikiMedia, 13, 22; © Jamie Smed/Flickr, 15; © Dmitry Argunov/Shutterstock, 17; © Lorie Shaul/Flickr, 19, 23; © Jose Breton- Pics Action/Shutterstock, 21; Cover, 1, 6, 12, 16, Jeff Bane; Various frames throughout, © Shutterstock images

Cherry Lake Press is an imprint of Cherry Lake Publishing Group.

Library of Congress Cataloging-in-Publication Data

Names: Pincus, Meeg, author. | Bane, Jeff, 1957- illustrator.
Title: Megan Rapinoe / Meeg Pincus ; illustrated by Jeff Bane.
Description: Ann Arbor, Michigan : Cherry Lake Publishing, 2021. | Series:
   My itty-bitty bio | Includes index. | Audience: Grades K-1
Identifiers: LCCN 2020005678 (print) | LCCN 2020005679 (ebook) | ISBN
   9781534168404 (hardcover) | ISBN 9781534170087 (paperback) | ISBN
   9781534171923 (pdf) | ISBN 9781534173767 (ebook)
Subjects: LCSH: Rapinoe, Megan, 1985---Juvenile literature. | Women soccer
   players--United States--Biography--Juvenile literature. | Soccer
   players--United States--Biography--Juvenile literature.
Classification: LCC GV942.7.R366 P56 2021 (print) | LCC GV942.7.R366
   (ebook) | DDC 796.334092 [B]--dc23
LC record available at https://lccn.loc.gov/2020005678
LC ebook record available at https://lccn.loc.gov/2020005679

Printed in the United States of America
Corporate Graphics

table of contents

About the author: Meeg Pincus has been a writer, editor, and educator for 25 years. She loves to write inspiring stories for kids about people, animals, and our planet. She lives near San Diego, California, where she enjoys the beach, reading, singing, and her family.

About the illustrator: Jeff Bane and his two business partners own a studio along the American River in Folsom, California, home of the 1849 Gold Rush. When Jeff's not sketching or illustrating for clients, he's either swimming or kayaking in the river to relax.

I was born in Redding, California. It was 1985.

I have many brothers and sisters. I even have a twin sister.

My sister and I loved to play soccer. Our brother taught us how to play.

What's your favorite thing to do?

I watched bold, strong women win soccer's **World Cup** in 1999. I wanted to be like them.

Who do you look up to?

I played soccer in college. I became a **professional** soccer player.

My team won an **Olympic** gold medal. Later, my team won the World Cup. We got a **ticker tape** parade.

Men's soccer teams are paid more. I don't think that's fair. I speak out for fair pay for all.

What would you speak out for?

My girlfriend plays professional basketball. We support **equal rights** for women in sports.

I was named best women's soccer player in the world in 2019.

I am a soccer superstar. I am an **activist**. I want everyone to be treated fairly.

What would you like to ask me?

2012

1980

↑
Born
1985

2019

2080

glossary

activist (AK-tiv-ist) a person who works to bring about change in laws or society

equal rights (EE-kwuhl RITES) laws that guard people from being treated unfairly

Olympic (uh-LIM-pik) relating to the Olympic Games, which are summer and winter contests for athletes from all over the world

professional (pruh-FESH-uh-nuhl) making money for working hard at something others do for fun

ticker tape (TIK-uhr TAYP) small pieces of paper that are thrown into the air at parades celebrating a person or group

World Cup (WURLD kuhp) the major contest that soccer teams from around the world compete in every 4 years

index